DATE DUE

MAY 23 1997	OCT 09 1998	JUN 09 2000
JUN 13 1997	OCT 30 1998	
SEP 19 1997	DEC 1998	SF 13
OCT 17 1997	FEB 03	OC 05 '01
NOV 20 1997	FEB 16 1999	OC 26 01
DEC 19 1997	SEP 17 1999	NO 09 '01
JAN 23 1998		AP 20 04
FEB 13 1998	NOV 00	
FEB 20 1998	DEC 17 1999	SE 07 '04
JUN 10 1998	FE 18 '00	9-24
SEP 23 199	MR 24 2000	16-25
		12-21-07

16-1-08

Swift as the Wind

For T.S.E.
His record-breaking sprint to the library
remains unchallenged to this day!
—B.J.E.

With gratitude to Paige for her vision and encouragement,
and to Craig for his steady, loving support
—J.C.

My thanks to University of California, Davis, scientist Timothy Caro, world authority on cheetah behavior, who generously shared with me his extensive research and who read my manuscript to ensure its accuracy.—B.J.E.

Orchard Books, 95 Madison Avenue, New York, NY 10016

Manufactured in the United States of America. Printed by Barton Press, Inc. Bound by Horowitz/Rae. Book design by Jean Krulis. The text of this book is set in 13 point Garamond Light. The illustrations are designer's gouache on Arches paper.

10 9 8 7 6 5 4 3 2 1

Library of Congress Cataloging-in-Publication Data
Esbensen, Barbara Juster.   Swift as the wind : the cheetah / by Barbara Juster Esbensen ; illustrated by Jean Cassels.   p.   cm.   Summary: Describes the physical characteristics and habits of the cheetah, fastest of the big cats.   ISBN 0-531-09497-9. — ISBN 0-531-08797-2 (lib. bdg.)   1. Cheetah—Juvenile literature. [1. Cheetah.]   I. Cassels, Jean, ill.   II. Title.   QL737.C23E735   1996   599.74′428—dc20   95-666

Swift as the Wind
THE CHEETAH

by Barbara Juster Esbensen   illustrated by Jean Cassels

ORCHARD BOOKS   NEW YORK

$\mathcal{H}$ow fast is fast? Many wild creatures use speed to catch their prey. The sleek river otter can propel itself through the water faster than any other freshwater mammal, and the loon can move underwater even faster than the otter. In the ocean, a bull killer whale has been clocked at almost thirty-five miles an hour. From the air, a peregrine falcon can sight its prey five miles away and swoop after it at a blinding two hundred miles an hour. On land, though, no animal can move as fast as a cheetah.

The fastest human runner—an Olympic gold medal winner—can sprint to a top speed of twenty-seven miles an hour. But a cheetah would pass that runner in a sixty-five-mile-an-hour blur. Some of these big cats may reach speeds of close to seventy miles an hour.

They can go at this furious pace for only about thirty seconds, but for that brief time, no animal anywhere on earth can outrun them. Although they are not nearly as heavy nor as strong as their relatives—leopards, jaguars, lions, and tigers—their incredible speed allows them to survive.

The tawny, black-spotted cheetah is a member of the cat family. Every cheetah has its own unique pattern of spots. Its golden eyes seem large in the small, triangular face. Running from the corner of each eye is a single dark line, like the track of a tear.

The cheetah's body is lean and muscular, with long, slender legs like a greyhound's. It has a long tail used for balance when the animal must make sudden, swift changes in direction during a chase. This elegant tail ends in a row of black and white stripes and is tipped with white.

Unlike its big cat cousins—and unlike the cats we have in our homes—the cheetah cannot pull in its claws to make a soft paw. Its claws are always ready, like a human runner's cleats, to grab the earth for traction. These claws allow the cheetah to shoot forward from a dead stop to a possible speed of fifty miles an hour in just two seconds.

Its heart, lungs, and vascular system are larger than normal for its size—another reason it can accelerate so fast. With their long legs and springy backbone, cheetahs can cover twenty feet with each bounding rush.

The voice of the cheetah is not like the voice of any other big cat. Cheetahs do not roar. They make a birdlike chirping sound, and they can growl and hiss. Sometimes they purr.

At one time, cheetahs flourished in Asia as well as in many parts of Africa. The name *cheetah* comes from the Hindu word *chita*, which means "spotted one." Now they are almost extinct, except in certain small areas of eastern and southern Africa.

Like all other cats, the cheetah has a good sense of smell and good hearing, and it has especially sharp eyesight. It will often climb to the top of a termite mound or rock or other high ground to survey the countryside. If a cheetah is hungry when it sees a group of prey animals, it will come down and begin to stalk them. Unlike other cats, cheetahs are not night stalkers. They prefer to hunt at dawn and at dusk when the air is cool on the African plains.

In Tanzania, female cheetahs hunt Thomson's gazelles in their Serengeti range, but in other parts of Africa, they favor impalas. The larger males will kill antelope, young warthogs, and wildebeests. During the dry season in southern Africa, cheetahs sometimes quench their thirst by eating a certain kind of juicy wild melon.

If there are tall grasses, the stalking cheetah glides among these. Its pale, black-spotted body is camouflaged in the moving, grassy patterns of shadows and light, and this allows the animal to get closer to the prey without being seen.

The cheetah cannot run at top speed for great distances because its terrific speed uses up a tremendous amount of energy. Its chances of catching the prey are best if the cheetah waits until it is less than one hundred feet away before hurling itself at the startled quarry. In this sudden burst of speed, all four feet may actually be off the ground. Slow-motion photography has shown that cheetahs are airborne half the time during a chase!

The cheetah streaks after the desperately zigzagging prey and knocks it down from behind, using a front leg to trip the animal and make it fall. Then it bites down on the animal's throat and cuts off its air supply.

At least half the time, a cheetah is not successful in the hunt. But if a kill is made, the cheetah will drag it to a bush or tree where there is some shade. Then the cheetah rests, exhausted from the chase. Sometimes it will wait for as long as a half hour before beginning to eat.

This half hour of resting time can be dangerous for the cheetah. Hyenas and lions often watch a cheetah make a kill and then rush in and take it for themselves. Hyenas travel in fierce roving packs and have a huge advantage against a lone cheetah. And the lion, of course, is four or five times larger than a one-hundred-pound cheetah. A cheetah trying to defend its kill would be risking its own life. Experts estimate that a cheetah may lose as many as one kill out of every ten to such enemies.

Cheetahs can mate at any time of the year, and about three months later the female gives birth. The female chooses some well-hidden, safe place for her lair. Perhaps she finds flattened grass under a bush or in a thicket of bushes. Sometimes she will give birth in the middle of a marsh. Cheetahs usually have litters of two to four cubs and can have as many as six.

Infant cheetahs weigh less than a pound and, like a house cat's kittens, are born with their eyes closed. When they are about nine days old, they can stand, and in another three weeks they are walking on steady legs and chirping for their mother like little birds. Their mother answers them with the same high-pitched chirping sound. Female cheetahs looking for a cub that has wandered away have been known to answer a bird's call, mistaking it for their own youngster's voice.

Baby cheetahs are under their mother's care until they are over a year old and have learned to hunt for their own food. She nurses them until they are six weeks old, and she needs to hunt every day so that she always has plenty of milk. Often she must leave them hidden in the lair while she trots off to look for prey. Because the herds of prey animals wander from place to place on the African plains, the mother cheetah must follow them. She is sometimes away from her cubs for an entire day. She usually returns to them each evening and stays with them during the night. Life can be very dangerous for the small cubs if they are alone and lions or hyenas are nearby.

When the cubs are six weeks old, they can join their mother at the kills, where they are under her watchful protection. Now they are eating meat and do not need to nurse as often. Young cheetahs may often spoil the hunt when they tag along with their mother. Just as she begins to edge forward for the attack, the cubs may sit straight up to take a look or may roll and tumble in the grasses, startling the herd into wheeling away.

When the cubs are six months old, their mother begins to teach them to hunt by releasing small prey in front of them. Even when the cubs are learning to hunt for themselves, however, their mother furnishes most of what they eat.

Cheetah young have only their mother to depend on for food and protection. In a group, or pride, of lions, there are many mothers to care for one another's cubs. If a lioness must leave her babies, another female will take over the duties of mothering them. Cheetahs bring up their young alone. The male cheetah has no part in raising them. A female cheetah's cubs would be in grave danger if anything happened to her. She hunts with her grown offspring until the youngsters wander off to look for mates. Then she is alone again.

After leaving their mother, male cubs from the same litter often form what is called a coalition and stay together for life. These territorial males hunt together, find mates, and stake out territories together. They do not tolerate other males that try to mate in the same area and will often have fierce fights with these single males. When female cubs leave their mother, they do not form groups with other females. They remain solitary until they have cubs of their own.

The gentle, mild-tempered cheetah is the only big cat that people throughout history have kept as a pet. Cheetahs are easy to tame, and for centuries they were the pampered hunting companions of pharaohs and maharajas. Pictures of beloved cheetahs were painted on the walls of Egyptian tombs. The ancient tomb of the pharaoh Tutankhamen held a funeral couch built in the shape of a cheetah, whose face had tear lines of blue crystal. In the fourteenth century, the traveler Marco Polo reported that Mongol rulers in Asia used cheetahs on deer-hunting expeditions.

Until the Endangered Species Act was passed in 1973, cheetahs were kept as pets by some private citizens in the United States. Today only wildlife parks and zoos are allowed to keep cheetahs in captivity. In the wild, their numbers are becoming fewer and fewer—maybe no more than ten thousand in the entire world. Scientists think that a cheetah's life span in the wild may be as short as seven years. However, in the safer environment of a wildlife park or zoo, adult cheetahs can reach the age of fifteen.

Researchers have found that lions kill many cheetah cubs. They kill so many, in fact, that scientists now believe that lions are the main reason there are fewer cheetahs in the wild. Where there are large lion populations, the number of cheetahs remains low. Cheetahs living far from lions are able to survive in greater numbers.

Another possible threat to the survival of cheetahs seems to be genetic. In testing the blood of many unrelated cheetahs from widely separated areas of central and southern Africa, researchers have found that they are almost all genetically identical. The DNA from these cheetahs is nearly the same, as though they were all identical twins to one another. This is a worrisome fact because genetic variation is important for the survival of a species. Without it, animals may not have the ability to throw off illnesses as easily. If a common feline disease should get a start in a cheetah population, the results could be very serious.

Continued study of cheetahs may give scientists a way to help them. Cheetahs in eastern Africa may show a genetic pattern slightly different from that of other cheetahs. Cheetah experts think that a breeding program between animals from that area and other groups may help the cheetahs develop a better immune system. This could make a difference in their ability to resist illnesses.

Above all else, we know that the world's human population is growing at a rapid rate. Land that used to be a natural habitat for certain animals is now being taken over by people. Cheetahs, like many wild animals, are threatened by this shrinking of their hunting grounds.

Cheetahs are the swiftest runners ever to exist on this planet. Today dedicated animal biologists are doing everything possible to help these unique and spectacular animals outrun the shadows of extinction that may be closing in on them.